Dear young people . . .

This book was edited by Christine Krzystofczyk with assistance from Marcia T. Lucey and Alan J. Hommerding. Design and layout by Christine Enault. Production manager was Deb Johnston. This book was set in Adobe Garamond, Arial, and Sheila. Printed in USA.

WLP 017140   ISBN 978-1-58459-742-1

Dear young people...

*Inspiration from Pope Francis
for Everyone*

Michael O'Neill McGrath, OSFS

World Library Publications

the music and liturgy division of J.S.Paluch Company, Inc.

800-566-6150 • wlpmusic.com

Table of Contents

Introduction

Even though the title of this book suggests that it is intended only for young people, I really have people of all ages in mind. It should really be called *Dear Everybody Who Is Young at Heart*, because they are exactly the ones to whom Pope Francis reaches out time and again in his tweets, homilies, and reflections. His words are the source for the quotes you see illustrated throughout the book.

As St. Francis de Sales used to say, "You get more flies with a spoonful of honey than a barrel full of vinegar." Pope Francis, who has completely captured the world's attention and affection, is living proof of that maxim. Simply put, he is a self-described sinner who is all about Jesus—a gentle and patient Jesus who loves all people of all faiths and cultures, and who wants nothing more than for each of us to be our best selves and live in peace.

I once had the great pleasure of bumping up against Pope Francis twice in one week! The first occasion was when I attended one of his weekly audiences, held every Wednesday morning in the gigantic piazza in front of St. Peter's Basilica. I didn't count heads, but there certainly appeared to be around eighty thousand people in attendance, which I was told is a typical number. Gray clouds and a persistent drizzle didn't dampen at all the excited energy and enthusiasm of the crowd, like a football game without the tailgating.

I stood with my group way in back of St. Peter's Square where we could observe the vast sea of brightly colored umbrellas and plastic rain ponchos. We chose a spot right next to the guardrail that marked off the route of the Popemobile.

With two hours to kill, I managed to sketch the entire scene unfolding before us in that mammoth piazza designed in the seventeenth century by Bernini, meant to represent the two arms of Mother Church reaching out to the world and holding us in, both at the same time. Pretty clever, that Bernini, I thought, as I let my sketching pen guide me along. Four centuries later, his genius still resonates.

At long last, the white Popemobile did indeed pass just a few feet in front of us, the good pope standing within, waving to all, smiling his familiar smile. While it was over in a flash, I did manage to get a nice shot of people's blurred hands holding up their cameras. But that doesn't matter to me in the least, because it is the moment that will stay forever in my heart and memory, the feelings generated by his palpable warmth and affection, which I was sure were directed at me.

Several days later, still in Rome, a small group of us was unexpectedly treated to another pope-spotting moment as we exited a shop where my sister was in search of a leather handbag. The shop was right around the corner from the Church of the Gesù, the mother church of the Jesuits, where, it just so happened, Pope Francis had been celebrating a special liturgy. (It was thoughtful of him to time the end of Mass with the end of our shopping spree.)

We waited for thirty minutes before he was whisked by, directly in front of us, in his little blue car, which gave me time to make a sketch of yet another crowd filled with excited anticipation at being so close to Pope Francis. While he didn't stop the car to say he recognized us from St. Peter's the other day, I was struck once again by his broad smile and genuine sense of affection. He actually radiates gentleness and joy, making it perfectly natural for me to call him Papa.

Joy is one of Pope Francis's defining characteristics. He preaches it by word and example. He reminds us time and again that even in the face of poverty, illness, war, and alienation, in the center of our broken hearts and through our lonely nights, Christians have joy and hope because the Good News of the gospel—Jesus' story—is also our story.

I hope, dear young people, that Pope Francis's love of life and hope for the future inspire you to do good for others and to work at building peace and justice in our painfully troubled world and Church. May you strive to become a living gospel of joy, a healing face of Jesus, a presence of peace for the whole world—beginning in your own little corner of it. —*Michael O'Neill McGrath*

Chapter 1

THE JOY OF
THE GOOD NEWS

A woman in Virginia who is an active member of a parish served by priests in my congregation, the Oblates of St. Francis de Sales, told me that she once shared the name of her parish with someone she had just met. That person derisively said, "Oh, you go to that Oblate 'feel-good' parish." I love it! As if feeling good in church is a bad thing. The sad reality is that a lot of folks feel that way. I hope I'm seated next to them at the heavenly banquet, when we're all "feeling good."

St. Francis de Sales used to say, "A sad saint is a sorry saint." Pope Francis has said similar things many times. In fact, he is considered the first pope in history to use the word translated as sourpuss. If we truly believe that we are made in the image and likeness of God, and that God never abandons us or leaves us alone, then how can we not be filled with joy, even when we are sad? Can you imagine spending eternity with a cranky God who is constantly checking the sinner-detection app on a heavenly tablet?

Remember, dear young people, that the God whom Jesus came to earth to tell us about, whom he called his Father in heaven, is all about mercy and love. Pope Francis has said that the confessional should not be a torture chamber. No one is more patient with us than God. St. Thérèse, the Little Flower, one of my favorite "BFFs" in heaven (and she could be yours, too), used to say that God has the worst memory of anyone she knew. And isn't that good news? In fact, the best news ever?

Each day in our world

Beauty is born anew,

It rises transformed through the storms of history.

Pope Francis

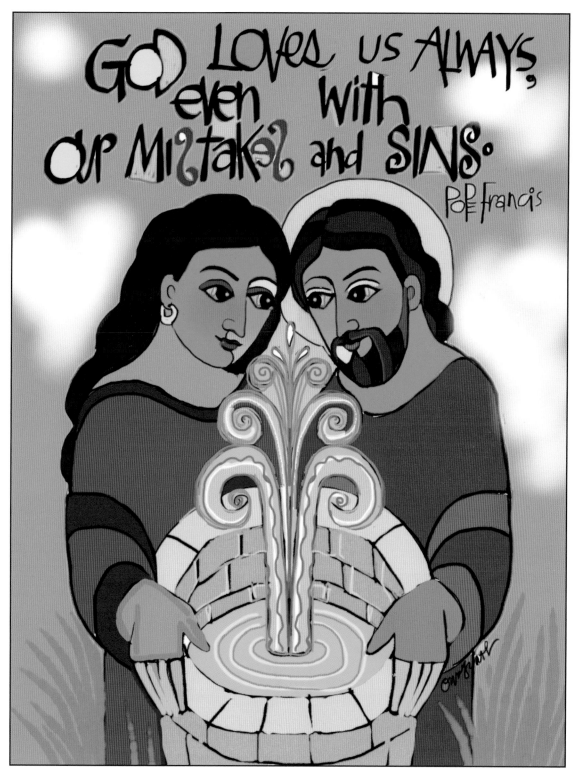

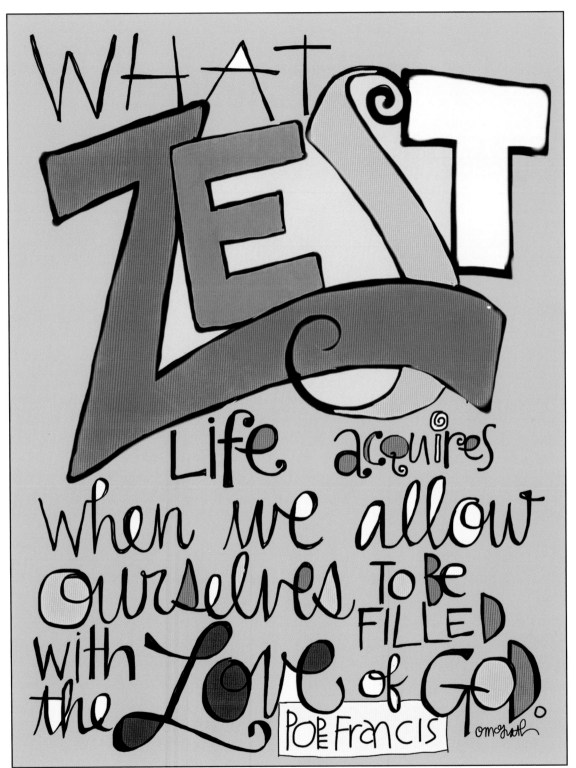

WHAT ZEST Life acquires when we allow ourselves to be filled with the Love of God.

POPE FRANCIS

Talking about God isn't about imposing beliefs, but rather about sharing the Joy of Faith.

Pope Francis

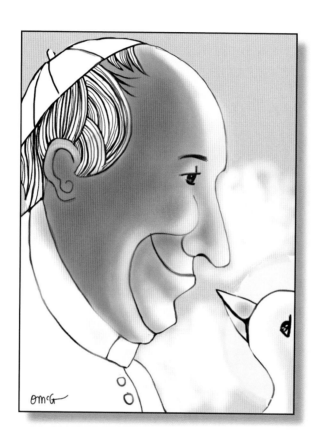

Chapter 2

JESUS

It's all about Jesus: everything through him, with him, for him, and in him. He's your doctor when you're sick, your counselor when you're confused. He's your mother and father when you're afraid, your brother and sister when you're lonely, your best friend when you need an ear. He is *you* whenever you are patient, gentle, and kind, especially to someone you may not particularly care for. You are the face of Jesus to me, whether you are male or female, young or old, fat or thin, gay or straight, or whatever combination of colors and cultures your ancestors came from—as long as your heart is full of goodness and right intentions. As St. Teresa of Ávila used to say, God has no hands on earth but yours to do the work of Christ. So, lend a hand, then give yourself a hand!

There is neither a Catholic Jesus nor a Lutheran Jesus, a Quaker Jesus nor a Baptist Jesus. Jesus is neither Republican nor Democrat, nor the official voice of any other political party. He's not even American. There is no hate group that has anything whatsoever to do with Jesus, even the ones who call themselves Christian. Jesus does not cause death and destruction as retribution, nor does he take sides at hockey games. Jesus, even in the midst of your sinfulness and weakness, opens his arms and embraces you. How can you hear Jesus' voice from the mouth of someone who puts you down, holds you back, or judges you for who you are or where you come from?

Take note, dear young people: Jesus just doesn't operate like that. And you can't pin Jesus down. He's like a cloud that way, a big, beautiful cloud that's always there, gently hovering above like a comfortable blanket. May the words and actions of Pope Francis awaken your senses to who Jesus is—and wants to be—in your life. Experience Jesus as he is to you, in you, for you, and through you.

Jesus breaks through the BORING CATEGORIES to which we try to limit Him.

Pope Francis

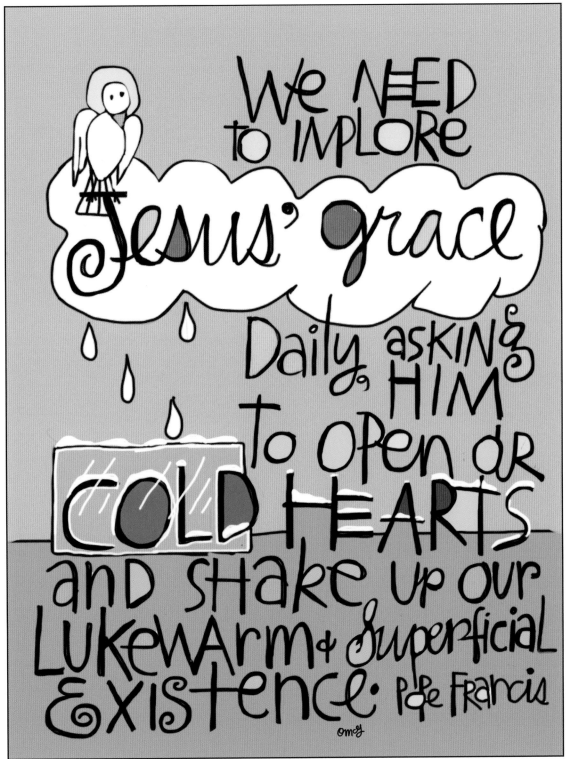

We need to implore Jesus' grace daily, asking Him to open our cold hearts and shake up our lukewarm & superficial existence. Pope Francis

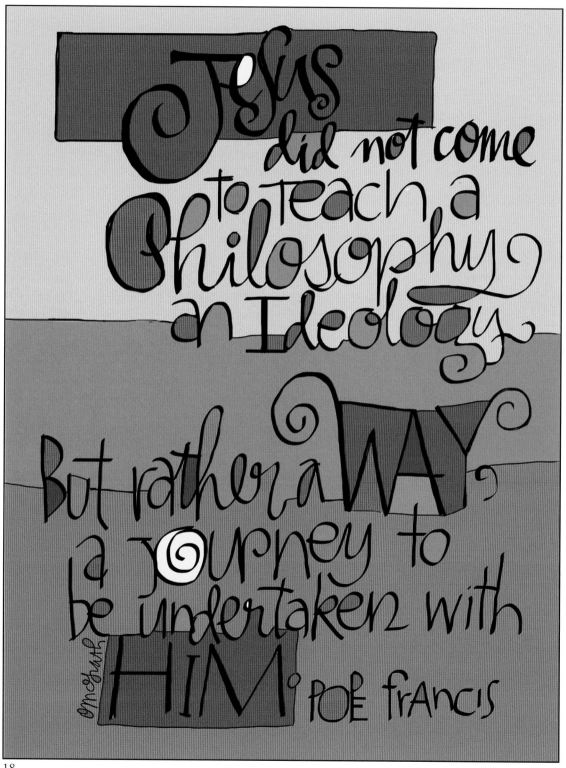

Jesus did not come to teach a Philosophy an Ideology

But rather a WAY, a journey to be undertaken with HIM. PoPe Francis

18

Chapter 3

DEAR YOUNG PEOPLE:
YOUTH, SCHOOL, AND FAMILY

Pope Francis seems to be eternally young at heart, an attitude that frequently emerges in his tweets and messages to young people around the world. He reminds us of the gift of education and how much he loved school because it broadened his horizons. He assures us that it is okay to ask questions and challenge the status quo, to be creative and joyful, to appreciate family.

He also reminds us time and again of the importance of families in our lives, which nowadays come in all sorts of styles, colors, and configurations. It feels to me as if we humans are finally growing closer to what had been sketched out in that inscrutable God-mind since the first days of creation: that when we look at each other, we are really seeing the inexhaustibly beautiful image and likeness of God right here on earth; that we are each a dwelling place for the Holy Spirit.

Pope Francis also challenges us to take a penetrating look at the place of ever-changing technology and social media in our homes and lives. He likes to point out that while these things are all tremendous blessings and gifts, they can never replace genuine human interaction, the times we actually see, hear, help, feed, and hug each other like one big, happy (and even at times dysfunctional) family.

So, dear young people, keep in mind what Pope Francis calls the three most important phrases in every home: "I love you." "I forgive you." "Thank you." He has been very clear about that, pointing out that our experience of loving family life (and I include here our church families) can and should be the same as our experience of God, the ultimate loving parent who is always at home with a light on, patiently awaiting our return.

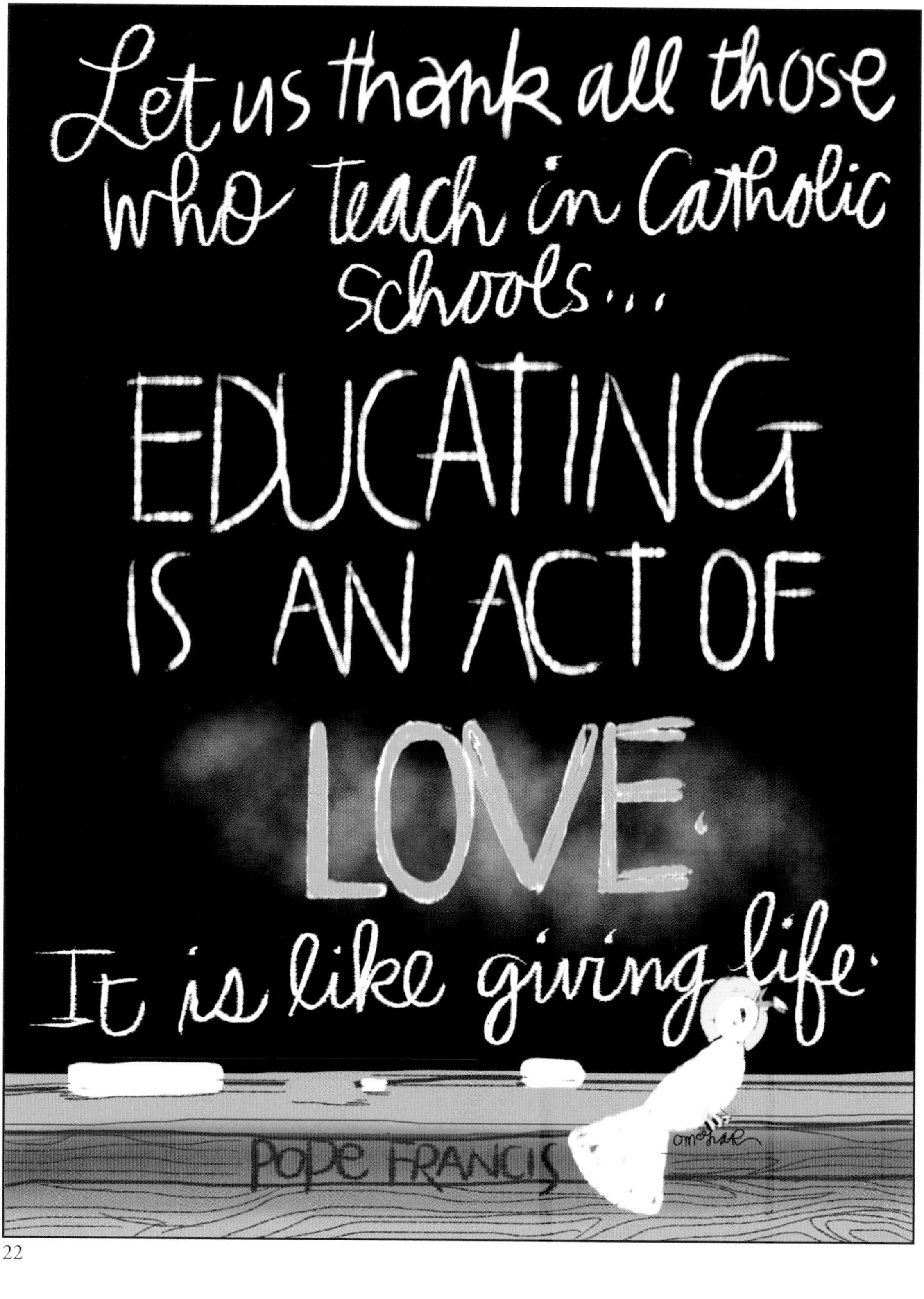
Let us thank all those who teach in Catholic schools...
EDUCATING IS AN ACT OF LOVE.
It is like giving life.
POPE FRANCIS

I have never forgotten my first grade teacher. She made me love ~~skool~~ school.

POPE Francis

24

To be friends
with G☀D
means to pray
with "simplicity,"

Like children talking
to their PARents.☺

Pope Francis

In our families we learn to Love and to recognize the Dignity of all especially of the ELDerly. Pope Francis

DEAR YOUNG PEOPLE, Do not be satisfied with a mediocre life. Be AMAZED by what is TRUE + Beautiful, WHAT IS of GOD.

POPE Francis

May the LORD keep us all young at heart.

Pope Francis

Chapter 4

THE CHURCH
IN THE MODERN WORLD

Fifty years ago, Pope St. John XXIII felt it was time for the Church to enter the modern world and see that the Holy Spirit is alive and well, ever challenging us to move forward. The Church, he said, can no longer be seen as a mere museum conserving dusty traditions. On his deathbed he said it wasn't the gospel that was changing, but rather the way we hear it. It seems to me that Pope Francis, a man who is such a huge fan of Pope John's that he canonized him, is taking up where John left off.

What is so exciting about Pope Francis is that so many people around the world have embraced him, not just Catholics. They witness his untiring determination to teach us all that our God is a God of mercy, creativity, and love, not cruelty and revenge. It is the vocation of every single one of us who is baptized in the Church, not just our religious leaders, to be living proof that God is alive and well.

Dear young people: Because the world—and the Church as well—belong to all of us, we must take loving responsibility for them. Pope Francis teaches us what Jesus has said all along: We must never tire of feeding the poor, tending the sick, clothing the naked, sheltering refugees and immigrants. We are the ones who must stop wars, end violence, protect the environment. And it is we who must swaddle the least of us, from crying babies to disabled adults, in loving hugs, proving that we can be spiritual, religious, and joyful all at the same time.

The Church is the House of the Father... Where there is a place for EVERYONE.

Pope Francis

the PAIN and the shame we feel at the sins of some members of the CHURCH, and at our own, must NEVER make us forget how many Christians are giving their lives in LOVE.

PopeFrancis

34

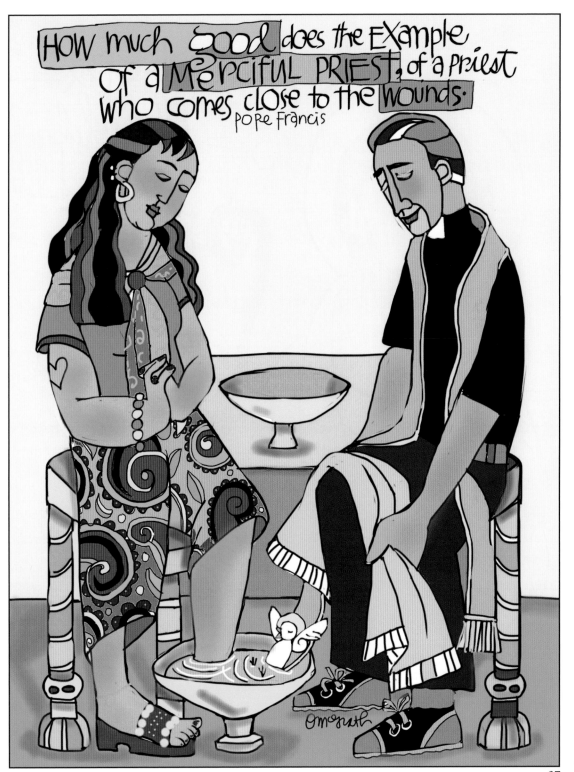

How much good does the example of a Merciful Priest, of a priest who comes close to the wounds. Pope Francis

Chapter 5

GOD, DISCIPLESHIP, WOMEN, AND MARY

Our Lady of Aparecida is the national patroness of Brazil, where her statue was miraculously caught in the nets of three fishermen in the River Paraíba in 1717. She is only three feet tall, but she is housed in the largest Marian shrine in the world. She is a Black Madonna, a feature important to her devotees because Brazil is a country that, like the United States, was built almost entirely on the backs of African slaves. Tiny as she is, Aparecida is flowing with a never-ending river of hope, grace, and the promise of peace and justice for the millions of pilgrims who drop by to visit her, the most famous of whom is Pope Francis.

Before he was pope, he held a meeting of all the bishops of Latin America in Aparecida because he wanted them to be in the company of such a little thing that is really quite extraordinary. If you are looking for Jesus, he says, just knock on his Mother's door. In her Magnificat, one of the most cherished canticles in church history, Mary points out the joyful good news that through her Son, Jesus, Almighty God reaches out to the lowly and the poor, lifts them up, and brings them hope and grace and all good things.

Dear young people, where I live, in the course of any given day and right outside my kitchen door, I witness poverty, homelessness, violence, and the ravages of addiction in beautiful people just like you, made in the image and likeness of God. And I find myself grateful to all the primary teachers of my faith, overwhelmingly women, who have taught me from the time I was a little boy—and continue to do so today—that all those tired faces in the margins of life (and there are way too many margins) are in reality the best places to meet Jesus all over again as if for the first time.

Mary, a simple girl from the country who carries within her heart the fullness of Hope in God.

— Pope Francis

41

In Mary's womb

God's hope took flesh.
Pope Francis

FEMININE GENIUS IS NEEDED in ALL expressions IN THE LIFE OF Society

Pope Francis

43

WE NEED A CHURCH CAPABLE OF REDISCOVERING THE MATERNAL WOMB OF MERCY

POPE FRANCIS

Mary is a sign of Hope for People who suffer the Birth pangs of Justice.
POPE Francis

Chapter 6

MERCY IN THE MARGINS

Who draws more attention than Pope Francis to the plight of the people in the margins: those who live in poverty; who are sick and elderly, disfigured and disabled, refugees and immigrants; victims of war and violence, human trafficking, and organized crime? As the pope says, we live in a world of wounded persons, and we should pray for the grace to weep over our indifference. Do we seek and find in them the very presence of Jesus?

Every day, I witness kindergartners skipping and hopping their way to Sacred Heart School across the street from my studio window. I see teenagers courageously determined to stay in school and avoid drugs and gangs. I see people of all ages and backgrounds who live on the streets or in tents by the highway, sleeping on flattened cardboard cartons every night in the parking lot of the cathedral house where I live with my community.

I also see some of you, dear young people: high school and college students from out of town who come to our fair city from near and far to play with those kids skipping to kindergarten, or to make bologna sandwiches by the boatload for the folks who sleep on the cardboard.

Pope Francis reminds us that the best place to encounter the living Christ is not in our comfort zones and shopping malls, but rather in the faces of all those who have been neglected and cast aside as inconsequential, a burden on society. It reminds me of the anonymous guy on the next page who knocked on our front door one cold afternoon in the winter from hell and asked for a blanket. If I could only find him to tell him that his grizzled face and toothless grin etched itself onto my artist's memory, warmed my heart, and inspired me to create an "icon"—for me, as true an icon of the face of Jesus as the one on Veronica's veil.

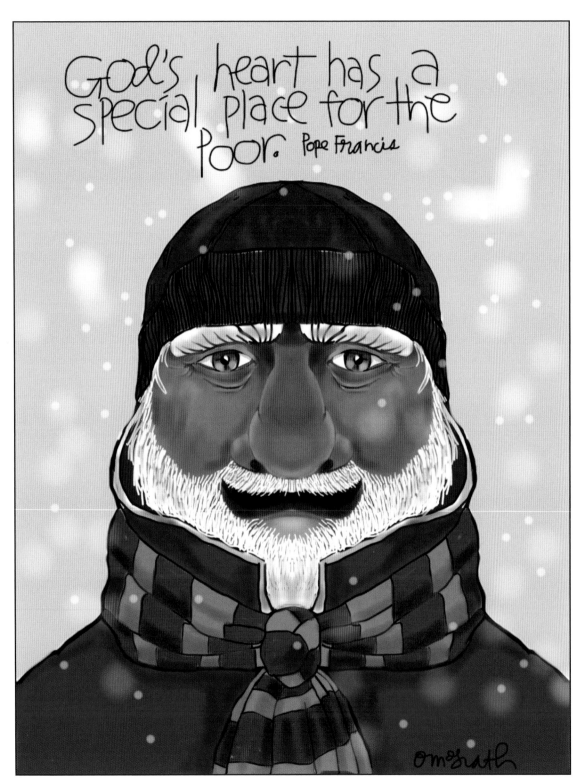

God's heart has a special place for the poor. Pope Francis

In the Poor and Outcast We See christ's Face.

Pope Francis

the WORSHIP the ancient GOLDEN Calf Has returned IN a NEW and RuTHLess guise... the culture of PROSPeRity Deadens us.

POpe Francis

51

The measure of the greatness of a society is found in the way it treats those most in need. Pope Francis

A society which abandons children and the elderly severs its roots and darkens its future. **POPE Francis**

Chapter 7

CREATIVITY AND PEACE

Father Tom Hagan is not only a good friend, he is a fellow Oblate of St. Francis de Sales and one of my great heroes and inspirations. He lives in Haiti, where over the years he has built schools, wells, and soup kitchens that have fed tens of thousands of people through the organization he founded called Hands Together. He barely survived the great earthquake that devastated Haiti in 2010 by jumping out a window before his house collapsed. Tom lives amid corruption, disease, and hunger, and yet he remains one of the calmest and funniest people I know.

Tom is just as attentive to what he learns from the people of Haiti as he is to what he teaches them. Even in the midst of gut-wrenching poverty and ongoing calamity, he tells me, the people of Haiti sing. He dances with the elderly ladies who come to the senior center for food. He feeds their bodies, and in return they fill his spirit.

Therein, my friends, lies the secret of a truly happy life: maintaining your inner peace in the midst of whatever challenges, or moments of challenge, life brings you. As I've gotten older and wiser, I've learned the truth behind St. Augustine's famous words, "Our hearts are restless until they rest in thee." St. Francis de Sales used to say that nothing is more important to us than our inner peace, that anxiety is the only thing worse than sin for the human soul. St. Teresa of Ávila said, "God cannot rest in an unquiet heart." And Mother Teresa taught that world peace begins right in our own homes, where we should never tire of saying "I love you" and "I forgive you."

Dear young people of all ages: Every single day in this world and Church of ours, we make personal choices in response to our individual losses and fears, as well as to war, violence, famine, and plague. One choice is to ignore our troubles, hoping that someone else will take care of them. Another is to recoil from them in depression and despair, or worse, self-medicate to avoid them. Yet another is to become part of the anger and hatred that created the trouble in the first place.

But I think I will go with Pope Francis and the saints across time, living and deceased, who remind me of the joy of the Good News, joy that is deeper than any broken heart could ever be. With joy comes peace. And with peace come beauty and the urge to create more beauty. And with beauty comes joy all over again in one great, far-reaching, all-encompassing circle of life and love.

Dear young people, *be* Good News today for someone who needs to hear it!

An Authentic faith... always involves a DEEP DESIRE To change the WORLD, to Leave this Earth somehow better than we FOUND it.

Pope francis

It is in giving ourselves, in emerging from ourselves, that we have true Joy.

POPE FRANCIS

be creative in order to achieve peace

Pope Francis

the Holy Spirit is the interior Master.

More than a Master of DOCTRINE, the Holy Spirit is a Master of Life.

Pope Francis

Notes

Brother Mickey McGrath, an Oblate of St. Francis de Sales, is an artist, author, speaker, and a big fan of the Holy Father. He creates weekly devotional art images, often using quotes of Pope Francis, which are featured on his Facebook page, Bro. Mickey O'Neill Mcgrath, OSFS. He currently lives and works in Camden, New Jersey. *Dear young people* is his seventh book with World Library Publications.